Exhibit Of Locomotives

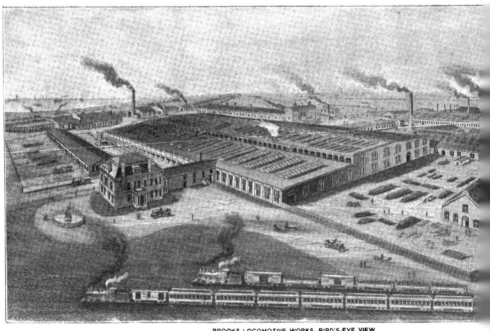

BROOKS LOCOMOTIVE WORKS, BIRD'S-EYE VIEW.

WORLD'S COLUMBIAN EXPOSITION.

CHICAGO, 1893.

Exhibit of Locomotives

M. L. HINMAN, . . PRESIDENT AND TREASURER.
F. H. STEVENS, . ASSISTANT TO THE PRESIDENT.
R. J. GROSS, ... VICE-PRESIDENT.
T. M. HEQUEMBOURG, ... SECRETARY.
D. RUSSELL, ... SUPERINTENDENT.
H. TANDY, . . . ASSISTANT SUPERINTENDENT.

MADE BY

BROOKS LOCOMOTIVE

DUNKIRK, N. Y.

U. S. A.

HISTORICAL SKETCH OF WORKS.

IN ISSUING this descriptive catalogue of our exhibit, it seems a suitab
give briefly a sketch of the origin and history of the establishment,
grown from a capacity of one locomotive per month in 1869, to the present
twenty-five (25) new locomotives per month are turned out.   Such an ac
thought will be of interest to our many friends, and this fact is our only ;
publishing it here.

In October, 1869, Mr. Jay Gould, then President of the Erie Railway, completed extensive shops at a more central location on the line, ordered t Dunkirk shops, which for many years had been the principal building and repa quarters of the company, should be permanently closed, and the machinery rem other locations. Mr. H. G. Brooks, at that time Superintendent of Motive Po Machinery of the Erie Railway, in order to prevent so great a misfortune fron on the home of his adoption as would result from the withdrawal of so man; workers from the place, and upon many men and their families to whom association he had become deeply attached, as well as to protect his own i which were all centered here, made a proposition to Mr. Gould for a lease of the sl machinery for the purpose of establishing the business of locomotive building in I

This lease was consummated, and in the following month of November th and machinery were transferred to the new Brooks Locomotive Works, business of locomotive building commenced in earnest. One locomotive in ea

months of November and December, 1869, was turned out, and the total prod

Works since that time has been 2,300 locomotives.

During the year 1883 the property, comprising twenty acres of l

permanent plant with additions and machinery — was purchased from the N

Lake Erie & Western Railway Company. The title passed to the Brooks Lo

Works, and the property became, as it now remains, a purely Dunkirk Com

entire stock being owned in this city, and the management of the Compa

exclusively in the hands of its owners, each of whom has his special depa

oversee. During all the years of prosperity and depression through which tl

have passed, the founders have had an implicit faith in the future, and ha

fastly carried forward the policy adopted at the beginning, of continuing the

ment and enlargement of the plant, and adding to the capacity and faciliti

Works. Extensive additions in the way of new buildings and machinery are no

made in all departments, which will very materially increase the capacity and ef

of the Works.

The present management, as given on the title-page of this catalogue, feel wa

in assuring their railway friends that the high character of the Brooks Locomoti·

in no wise be lessened, and that in view of the additions and improvements

progress and to be made in all departments of the Works, we will be foun

abreast of the times in our practice in locomotive building.

Dunkirk, N. Y., May 1, 1893.

ANNOUNCEMENT.

O N APPLICATION of intending purchasers we are prepared to submit
specifications and estimates for any pattern of locomotives not illust:
referred to in this catalogue, the principal dimensions and features being furnished
build to the specifications of Railway Companies or others.

In the construction of our locomotives the material used is the best of its kind,
details are accurately finished to standard gauges and templates kept for that purp
the view of their being interchangeable on all locomotives of the same class.

This feature we guarantee, and as we carry at all times an ample stock of parts liable to depreciation in service, we are thus enabled to fill promptly, or with possible delay, orders of that kind. The advantages of this system will be apparen way officers, as it enables the users of our locomotives to keep on hand for use at required, duplicates of any parts worn out or broken, or if preferred to order fro wire or mail required duplicates of any parts, and avoid the otherwise necessari expense of making drawings and patterns, and maintaining a force of skilled for the production of such parts; as with our experience and facilities for this work we can produce them more economically and of better uniform quality tha done by any except the largest and best equipped railway shops.

Our facilities for the construction of locomotive boilers and tanks are unsurpa we invite the correspondence of parties desiring to purchase these parts for the locomotives in their own shops.

The locomotives illustrated in this catalogue are arranged for use of b

coal for fuel. Should locomotives of these classes be required to burn anthra

or other fuel, all the necessary modifications would be made for that pu

some classes the firebox would be essentially lengthened. This addition woul

somewhat the total weight of the locomotive, which weight would come almos

on the drivers.

In the delivery of locomotives it is our practice to send a competent enginee

each locomotive in service on the tracks of the purchaser, and he will remain

performance is satisfactory to the person authorized to receive and receipt for the

Proposals for the construction of locomotives will be understood to co

delivery on track or free on board cars at our Works, unless otherwise specificall

the contract; but we will include delivery at destination when required, if the sa

reached by rail or vessel, and for foreign shipment free on board vessel at tide wa

Parties writing us for proposals, or ordering locomotives will please fu particulars as to gauge and maximum curvature, grades of track and weight o type of locomotive required, diameter and stroke of cylinders, diameter of boilei arch, length of firebox, fuel to be used, height of stack from top of rail, capacity gallons, lettering, numbering and painting.

We solicit your correspondence.

BROOKS LOCOMOTIVE W(

DUNKIRK, N. Y., U. S. A.

MAY 1, 1893.

SPECIFICATIONS.

TEN-WHEEL PASSENGER LOCOMOTIVE

CLASS 19. D.

ENGINE.

GAUGE, ... 4

FUEL, ... BITI

WEIGHT IN WORKING ORDER, ...

WEIGHT ON DRIVERS IN WORKING ORDER, ...

RIGID WHEEL BASE, ...

DRIVING WHEEL BASE, ...

TOTAL WHEEL BASE, ...

DIAMETER AND STROKE OF CYLINDERS, ...

DIAMETER OF DRIVING WHEELS, ...

DIAMETER OF BOILER, ...

LENGTH AND WIDTH OF FIREBOX, ... 11⸱

TENDER.

COAL CAPACITY, ...

CAPACITY OF TANK, ...

ENGINE AND TENDER.

TOTAL WHEEL BASE, ... 52

BROOKS LOCOMOTIVE WORKS,

DUNKIRK, N.Y.

U. S. A.

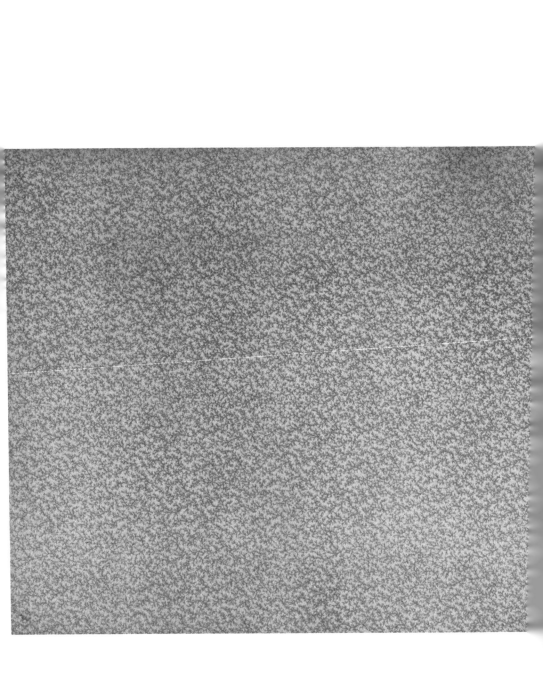

Lightning Source UK Ltd.
Milton Keynes UK
UKHW020626260722
406393UK00005B/832